How to Umpire Baseball and Softball

An Introduction to Basic Umpiring Skills

Steve Boga

For information about special discounts and bulk purchases, please contact Steve Boga at
707-869-1515
or
lifestories@memoirwritings.com

Cover photo courtesy of *Santa Rosa Press Democrat*.

Acknowledgments

Special thanks to Bill Kinnamon, Nick Bremigan, and John McSherry for elevating my game at the umpire school and voting to give me a job in professional baseball.

To Charlie Williams, my partner for two of my three seasons in organized baseball, both on and off the field. Without you, I never would have made it through the 1977 Texas League season.

Thanks to Jerry Klonsky for giving me the freedom to teach umpires my way.

And to Elaine and Blake Webster for breathing new life into this book project.

I'm indebted to Jim Whelly, Carl Hamilton, Tim Hallahan, and seventeen investors for making possible our instructional video, "You Be the Judge, An Introduction to Basic Umpiring Skills."

Maybe my greatest debt is to my first mentor, Willie Rossi, who taught and encouraged me, and finally pushed me off to umpire school.

Finally, I'm indebted to countless instructors and partners for their tips and support. And to thousands of students for making thousands of mistakes and allowing me, at least, to learn from them.

Author's Note

In 1972 I moved to Santa Rosa, California, to attend Sonoma State University and earn a teaching credential. Little did I know that I would soon be teaching umpiring skills.

Needing part-time work, I responded to a want-ad placed by the local officials association. Two years later, I was umpiring anything I could get, including high-school and summer-league baseball, and fastpitch and slowpitch softball.

In my third season, my mentor, Willie Rossi, said to me one day, "You should go to the umpire school. You could make it."

Until 1975, anyone aspiring to umpire in the Major Leagues had to attend a month-long umpire school in Florida. That year, a school opened in Reseda, California, north of Los Angeles. I took it as a sign and enrolled. Did well; got a job in the minors.

After two seasons in the California League and one in the Texas League, I was advancing as quickly as any umpire in

professional baseball. But I knew I couldn't go on. Although I loved the three hours on the field—still the best I've ever been at anything—I grew to hate the 21 hours off the field. That season in the Texas League was a six-month grind away from loved ones, an endless array of hotels, restaurants, and dressing rooms, interspersed every three or four days with a grueling road trip to Little Rock or Tulsa or San Antonio.

I quit professional baseball, but I was at the peak of my skills and had no intention of quitting the game. For the next dozen years I umpired major college baseball, including the Pac 10, and world-class fastpitch softball.

Meanwhile, I taught others to umpire, running countless indoor and outdoor training sessions. Over the years I created and refined a list that I call:

"*The skills and qualities needed to become the best umpire who ever lived*"

What follows is the product of that analysis—and of years of experience witnessing, and making, most of the mistakes described here.

Enjoy. And remember, as the book title says: Umpiring is the best seat in baseball, but you have to stand.

TABLE OF CONTENTS

TABLE OF CONTENTS

Section II

Photo Courtesy, ©AP

APPEARANCE

The Old Days: In July 1936, during a scorching heat wave, Ford Frick authorized Major League umpires to remove their coats and work in shirt sleeves. Still, well into the sixties, umpires continued to dress quite formally—black suit, black tie, white shirt.

Although the umpires' dress code has loosened considerably, appearance is no less important today than it once was. It's the first thing people notice—and first impressions stick.

Avoid: white socks, non-black shoes, colored belts, garish belt buckles, hats with insignias, wrinkled clothes, and unsafe equipment. Wear your shin guards and chest protector beneath your clothing, not on the outside. Never turn your hat backward or wear mismatching socks.

Even your conduct on the field can enhance or detract from your appearance. Don't smoke, drink beer, yuck it up with ballplayers, or carry an I-Pod. Look serious, sharp, and sincere.

POSITIONING

The Old Days: In the earliest days of baseball, umpires worked alone and made calls from the stands. By the early 20th Century, umpires had moved onto the field, first a plate umpire, then soon a partner, a "field" or "base" umpire, which created new positioning challenges.

Now let's review the static (before the pitch) positioning of the base umpire in the two-man system.

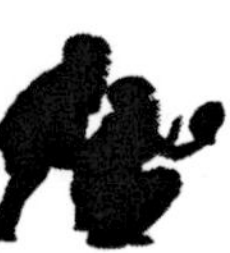

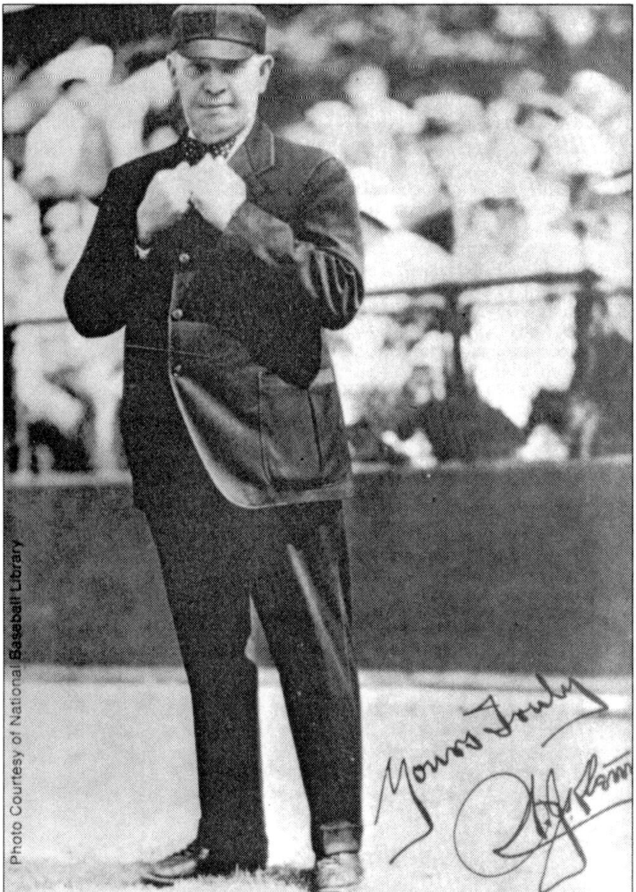
Photo Courtesy of National Baseball Library
Yours Truly

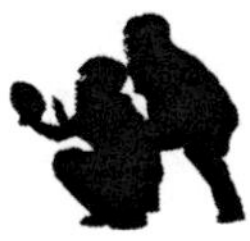

Baseball and Softball: Bases Empty

In all baseball and softball, with nobody on base, the base umpire sets up in foul territory, well behind the first baseman.

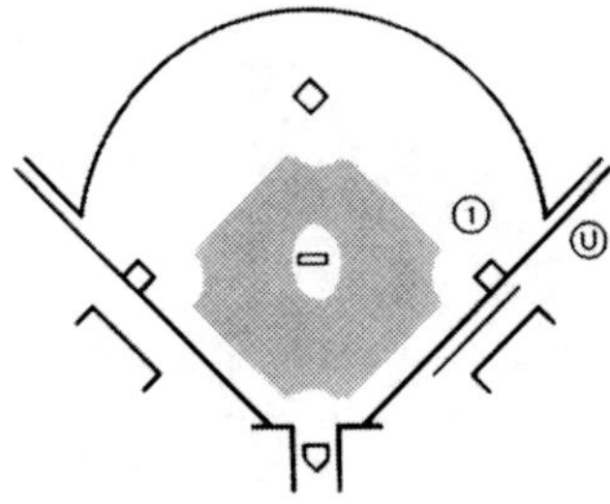

From here, you will get inside whenever the ball is hit to the outfield. Once inside the imaginary baseline between first and second, and at about the same time the batter-runner touches first, do a pivot, a three-step move that briefly opens you to first base. As you pivot, look to see: a) did the batter-runner touch first? b) did the first baseman obstruct the batter-runner? Then find the ball, and be ready to take the batter-runner into second, or back to first in case of a play there.

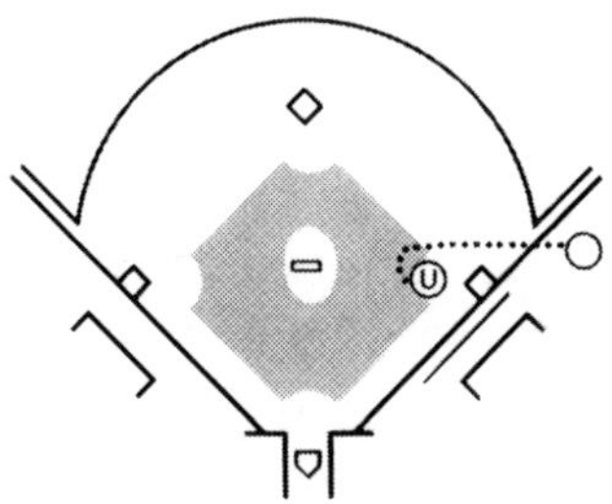

When the ball stays in the infield, the base umpire remains outside. On balls hit to the left side, move into fair territory and set up 12-15 feet from the bag, approximately 90 degrees from the line of the throw.

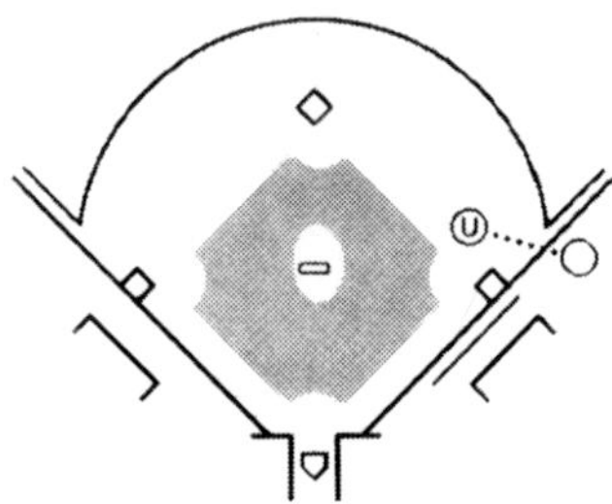

On balls hit to the right side, especially if the second baseman moves to his left, set up in foul territory, still looking for that 90-degree angle.

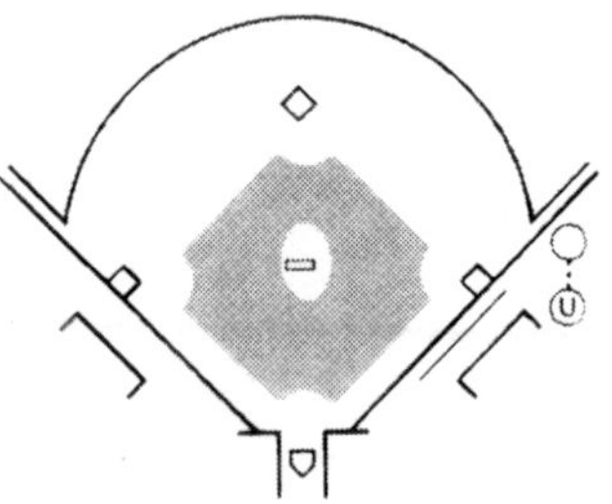

Baseball: Runner on First

The base umpire sets up behind the pitcher's rubber, just to the first-base side of an imaginary line between the rubber and second base.

On balls hit to the outfield, turn and face the outfield, retreating toward the pitcher's rubber to maximize peripheral vision. Be ready to take either the runner or the batter-runner into first or second.

On balls hit to the infield, the base ump is responsible for calls at all three bases, including both ends of any double play.

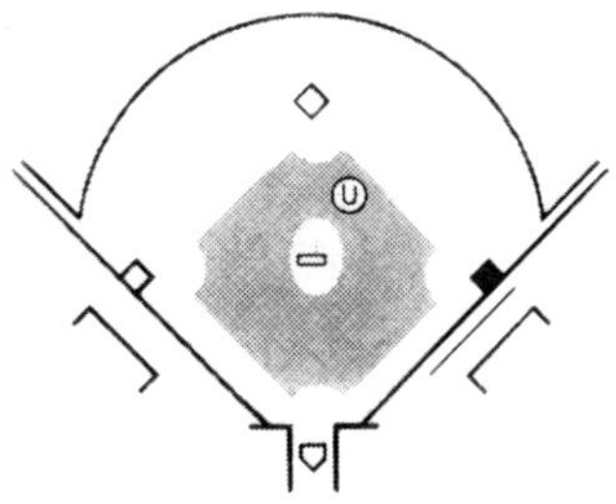

Baseball: Multiple Runners on Base

Any other combination of runners takes the base umpire to the other side—the third-base side—of the imaginary line.

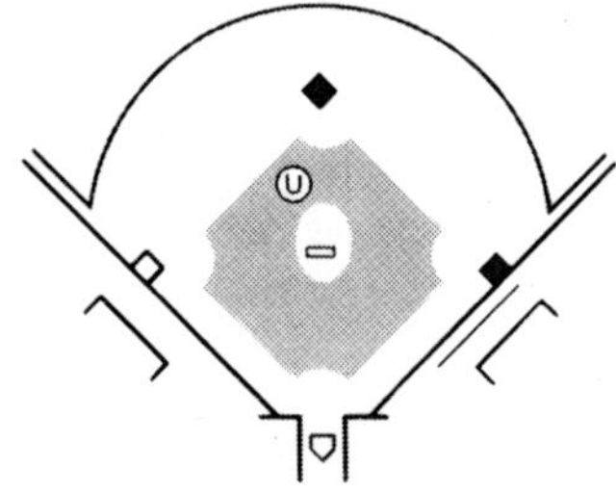

Little League Baseball and Softball: Runner on First

Here, the base ump always sets up outside the baselines. Find a spot behind the second baseman, to one side or the other. From there, you should be able to see the pitcher, batter, and runners.

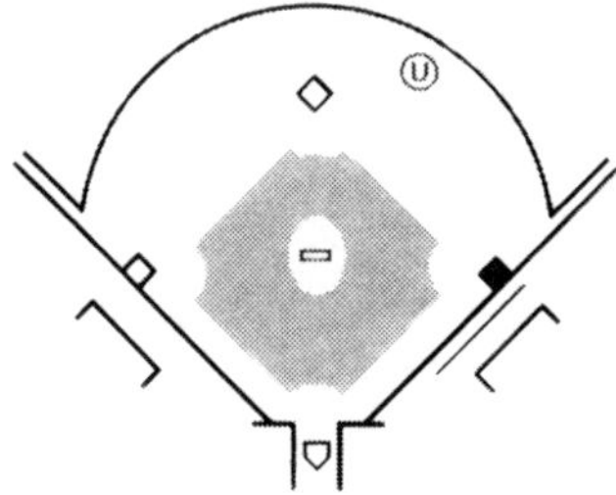

When the ball is hit to the outfield, get inside the baselines, pivot, and face the ball. Glance at the runners touching first and second, watch for possible interference, read the play (good anticipation), and move into position to make a call at first or second. If necessary, take the batter-runner all the way to third base.

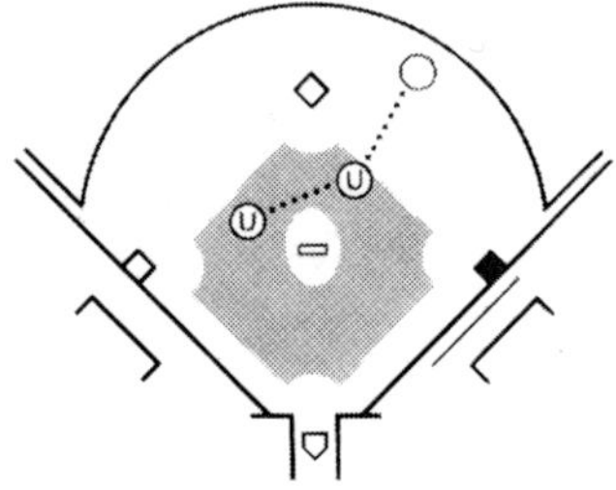

Little League Baseball and Fastpitch Softball: Multiple Runners on Base

In Little League and fastpitch softball (but not in slow-pitch), the base umpire may assume a third position. With multiple runners on, or a runner on second only, or third only, set up behind the shortstop, to one side or the other. Make sure you can see the pitcher, batter, and runners.

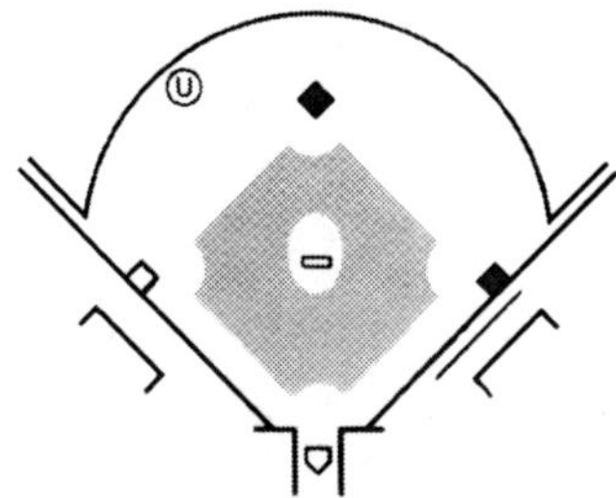

Plate Umpire: No Runners on Base

At all levels of baseball and softball, whenever the batted ball stays in the infield, the plate umpire exits to the left of the catcher and moves up the first-base foul line. If you get halfway, you are the Pete Rose of umpiring. Most important, you're in a better position to help your partner if the throw takes the fielder off the bag or there's a sweep tag.

Note: Don't make a call until the base umpire asks you for help.

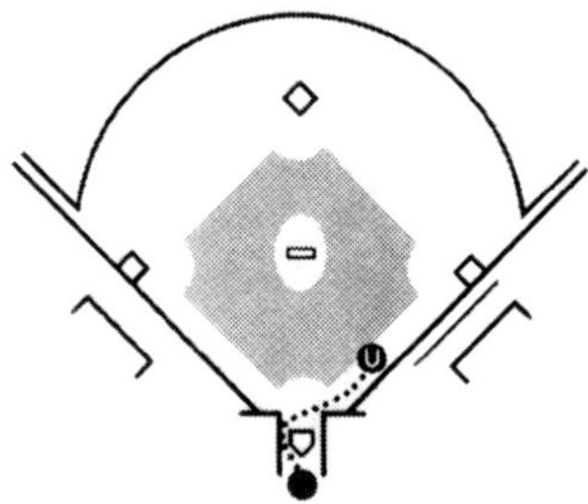

When the ball goes to the outfield, the plate umpire exits to the left of the catcher and moves out into fair territory, generally toward the ball but at an angle to rule on the catch.

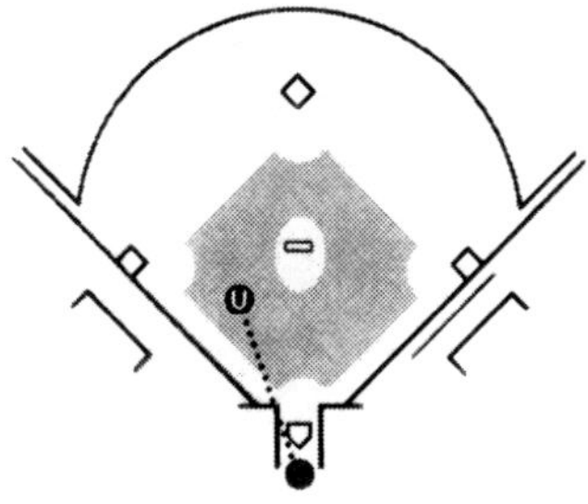

Plate Umpire: Runner on First

At all levels, whenever the ball is hit to the infield, the plate umpire exits left of catcher and starts toward third, anticipating a possible play there. If the out is made at second, eliminating the lead runner, reverse direction and move toward first, ready to a) help out there if asked, or b) rule on a overthrow into dead territory and, if necessary, award bases.

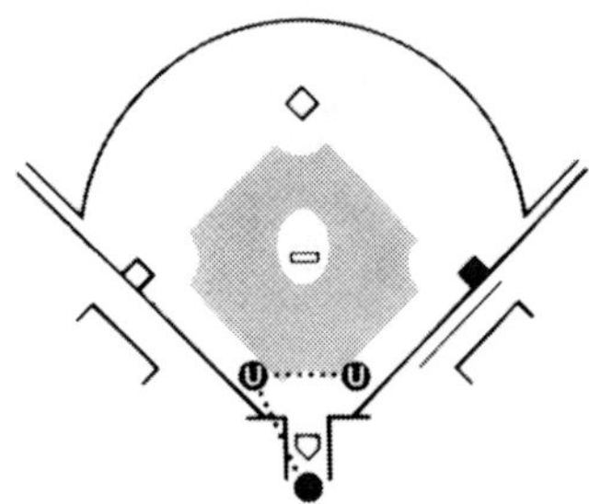

If the ball is hit to the outfield (or to the infield and the out is not made at second), be prepared to take the lead runner into third.

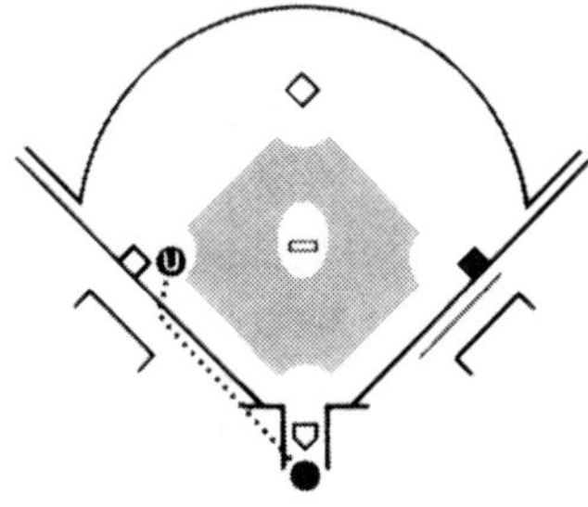

Plate Umpire: Multiple Runners on Base

When anticipating a play at home, the plate umpire should exit left of catcher, remove the mask, and move into foul territory on the third-base side of home.

In this situation, whether the ball is hit to the infield or outfield, the base umpire makes all calls at third base.

Exception #1: If the lead runner is clearly going to score, the plate umpire may move toward third, glancing over his shoulder to see the lead runner touch home plate. If he gets a good jump (anticipates well) and calls his partner off, he may make the call on the following runner at third.

Exception #2: In slowpitch softball, the plate umpire makes all calls at third if the ball stays in the infield.

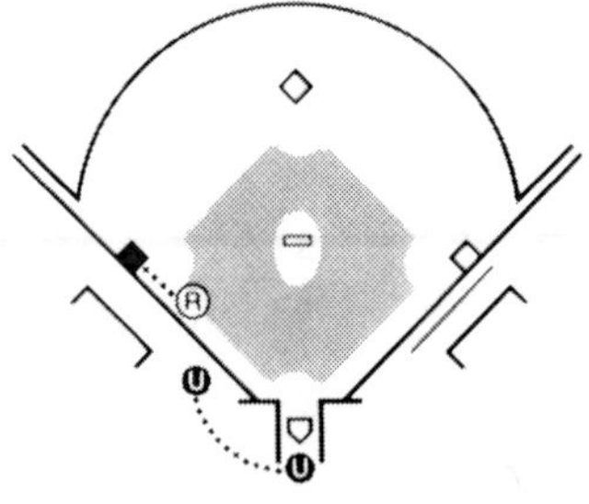

One-Umpire System

Umpiring a baseball or softball game without a partner is easy in one respect: there's no debate about coverage. The plate umpire makes all calls.

- Starting from the usual position behind the catcher, exit from the catcher's left every time the ball is hit.

- With no runners on and a ground ball to the infield, hustle out in front of the plate, heading roughly toward the second baseman to get an angle on the call at first.

- Positioning for calls at third and home is the same as in the two-umpire system. In addition, however, the solo umpire must be prepared to make the call on a following runner at second or even back at first.

ANTICIPATION

The Old Days: One day, with the umpires working two-man mechanics, and a runner on second, batter Johnny Moore hit a grounder to the shortstop, who fielded it and cocked to throw to first. Base umpire Larry Goetz, anticipating that the throw would indeed go to first base, turned and faced the bag. The batter-runner was still two steps away when Goetz heard what he thought was the sound of the ball pounding into the first baseman's glove. He calmly signaled out and was surprised when Moore exploded.

"Larry," Moore said, mustering his composure, "I feel I have a right to argue. The first baseman doesn't have the ball. They made the play at third instead."

Umpire Goetz had made a rookie mistake. He anticipated (guessed) that the shortstop would throw to first. By failing to see the shortstop release the ball, Goetz looked about as bad as an umpire can look.

Of course, umpires properly anticipate all the time. Goetz was not wrong to anticipate the throw going to first—that was the most likely play. But he was wrong to commit all his attention to first, ignoring a possible play elsewhere.

Adopt this as your mantra: "Watch the ball, glance at the runner." And always see the fielder release the throw.

In sum, there is good anticipation and bad anticipation. **Do not anticipate** out or safe, ball or strike. **Do anticipate** how a play will develop and where to go on the field.

Once the ball is hit, the umpire with good instincts will "read" the play and anticipate where the next throw will go. By hustling to get a few steps closer to the play or to improve your angle, you will impress others with your commitment and give your good judgment free reign.

VOICE

The Old Days: For decades, custom dictated that the umpire remain mute when "calling" balls. If he was fooled on the pitch or swallowed his gum or drifted off—it was a ball. But silence is not good salesmanship.

Say you're the plate umpire in a tight game: bottom of the ninth, two outs, 3-2 on the batter. The next pitch is knee-high and—in your estimation—a half-inch outside. You should:

a. Say nothing.
b. Say "ball" loud enough for the catcher and batter to hear.
c. Stay in your crouch (baseball and fast-pitch softball) and shout out "ball."
d. Call it a strike—it was close enough.

It's "c" in a landslide. Although the strike call, with its accompanying arm action, grabs our attention, the ball call is just as important.

Take the example above—what if that ball-four call walks in the winning run? How best to sell that call, to communicate to players, coaches, and fans that you saw it and got it right?

Stay locked in behind the catcher and bellow out the call.

Whether calling balls/strikes or outs/safes, the closeness of the pitch or play determines the volume of your voice. The closer it is, the louder your call. If the runner is safe by two steps or the pitch hits the backstop on a fly, you have nothing to sell. Save the flair for the knee-high corner pitches and the bangers on the bases.

FLAIR

The Old Days: The first umpire renown for his flair was Emmett Ashford, who also happened to be the first black umpire in the Major Leagues. Only five-foot-six and stocky, he was as agile as a dancer, as emphatic as a mime. "The only umpire they ever paid to see," said American League umpire Bill Kinnamon.

Ashford played to the crowd, receiving applause even for his distinctive style of dusting off home plate: five lightning-quick whisks, ending with a high twisting flourish of the dusting hand and a kick of the right foot. In the Dominican Republic, where Ashford worked winter ball, they called him "Pataditas"—Little Kicks.

After Ashford, there was Ron Luciano, who gained notoriety for his on-field antics, which included "finger-shooting" runners out on the bases and unleashing a flurry of maniacal safe calls.

Many view the showmanship of Ashford and Luciano as behavior more appropriate to the circus. They subscribe to the belief that the best-officiated game is one where you don't notice the umpires. Anonymity is an umpire's greatest reward.

That said, close plays demand salesmanship. It's not enough to be right—you have to persuade others that you are. Flair helps you achieve that. The closer and more important the pitch or play, the more flair you should bring to the call.

On the bases, square off to the play and keep your head still while you watch the catch or tag.

The safe call should be a high, wide, horizontal sweep of the arms. Synchronize the motion with one word: "Safe!" To signal out, thrust the right arm (never the left) into the air, snapping off a fist while crying, "He's (or "she's") out!" Sell close outs by coming over the top or punching the air for greater emphasis. Watch accomplished umpires and imitate what you like.

A big part of "selling the call" is the pizzazz umpires bring to the game. Flair: it's the polish on the gem of umpiring.

ATTITUDE

The Old Days: Bill Klem, who umpired in the Major Leagues for forty years, never addressed players by name, only by position. If the hitter squawked once too often, he would occasionally call a third strike that just missed the corner (not recommended). When the batter complained that he'd missed that one, Klem responded, "Ah, shortstop, but you missed the first two."

At times he'd retort, "If I'd had your bat in my hands, I wouldn't have."

After Klem retired, he said in an interview: "At the end of my career I could only see with one eye, but I could still umpire. I wasn't surprised because I never thought eyesight was the most important thing in umpiring. The most important things are guts, honesty, common sense, a desire for fair play, and an understanding of human nature."

In a word: Attitude.

It mostly comes into play when confronted by a beefing ballplayer. Umpire Bill Dineen was working first base one day when player-manager Jimmy Dykes took a long lead off first, then lapsed into a daydream. A snap throw from the catcher awakened him and he dived desperately back to the bag. Before Dineen could make his call, Jimmy was screaming, "I made it! I made it!"

Dineen, fist already pointed skyward, looked down at Dykes. "You certainly did, Jimmy," he said soothingly, "but what detained you?"

Dineen and other umpires have learned that sometimes you can defuse tension with humor—and that anger is usually counterproductive. When I began umpiring high school baseball, the president of our association was a cop. And he umpired like a cop, which meant he was always in trouble.

In 1975, I was umpiring in the minor leagues, California League, A-ball. One day after a game, Lee Mazzilli walked off the field with me. He said, "You know, you and Charlie (Williams) are the only umps in the league we don't argue with."

"Oh, why is that?" I waited for him to praise our superior judgment.

Instead, he said, "When those other crews make a call, they look at you in a way that just makes you want to yell at them."

He was talking about attitude.

Former National League president Warren Giles said that umpires should be "quick to think, slow to anger." Good advice, that. Even though others may lose their heads, umpires must hold to a higher standard. Don't let a childish player drag you down to his level.

Jerry Dale, former National League umpire, once did a study of umpire personality types for a master's thesis. Major League umps showed up as "highly aggressive, assertive, argumentative, stubborn, extroverted, and talkative." They were also "strong-willed, thick-skinned, and forceful."

When faced with an argument, the umpire must be able to stand his ground, to verbally defend himself. But if your goal is to make the grieved party walk away, it's sometimes best to let him have the last word. You should not let the argument get personal or prolonged—admittedly subjective areas—but the official who always insists on having the last word is heading for a high ejection rate.

An umpire's attitude toward his or her partner is also important. Arbiters who enjoy a reputation as "an umpire's umpire" support their partners to the end. Treat them with the respect you would accord any teammate, for that is what they are. Your only teammate(s). Learn your partner's name, have good eye contact and communication, be sensitive and supportive.

TIMING

The Old Days: Umpire Beans Reardon once signaled "out" and hollered "safe" on Richie Ashburn sliding into third. When Ashburn demanded an explanation, Beans thought of one: "It's true that you heard me call you safe. But it's equally true that thirty thousand fans saw me call you out. Ergo, yer out!"

What happened to Beans, a breakdown in timing, happens to every umpire who works long enough.

When timing breaks down, it tends to be too quick, not too slow. Some people seem to be born with an innate ability to "let the play happen." Fortunately, for the rest of us, it's a skill that can be learned.

When teaching on-field umpire clinics, I found this drill worked to cool overheated timing. On plays at first base, I would stand next to the student-umpire, wait for the sound of the ball smacking the first baseman's glove, then ask, "What was it?" Only then was the umpire permitted to make the call. If her voice overlapped mine, the timing was too quick.

All other things equal, slower timing means better judgment. The nature of baseball demands that umpires make calls quickly—but not immediately. A 90-mph pitch takes about a half-second to reach the catcher's glove. An event of such short duration cannot be watched, analyzed, and judged by the human brain with instantaneous precision. Follow the ball hitting the glove with a distinct, discernable pause while remaining in a neutral position, then explode into the call.

The best way to reveal timing problems is to videotape umpires-in-training. As the ball hits the glove, and for several frames thereafter, the umpire's head should be steady—"locked in." We get no clue what the call will be. If the umpire starts the call in the video frame in which the ball is hitting the glove, the timing is much too quick.

During the pause, your mind should be free of expectations. Don't think "out" or "safe" or even "wait." In time, you will train yourself to wait unthinkingly.

Of course, even veteran umpires occasionally have their timing go south. It happened to me in 1977, El Paso, the Texas League. It was near the end of the season and I knew the players' skills. The batter hit a slow roller to third baseman Carney Lansford, who charged and fielded the ball barehanded. As I moved into position to make the call at first, an unsolicited thought popped into my mind: "The batter-runner leads the league in steals." Then a second thought: "They're never going to get him. They're never going to get him."

Bang-bang—they got him!

"Safe!" I cried.

I had broken a cardinal rule. My "empty" mind had filled with unwanted thoughts, which had in turn corrupted my ability to react to the play. I had, at the subconscious level, made up my mind before the play happened.

Bad anticipation.

BASEBALL INSTINCT

An umpire is like a judge: We examine a body of facts- the evidence—and reach a decision. The difference is, umpires can't "sleep on it." We must render a decision in about a second (as opposed to a split-second). Clearly, instinct is more important than intellectualizing.

Baseball instinct is something we're born with to one degree or another. Still, we can refine those instincts, our feeling for the "inner game." Start by studying the Men in Blue. Analyze and, when appropriate, imitate.

Unfortunately, most people notice umpires only when we get in trouble. Kids grow up watching the game from the viewpoint of a fan or player. They may develop the instincts of a great shortstop but rarely those of a great umpire.

If you want to excel as an umpire, you must develop an eye for umpires. When you attend a game, fight the urge to watch the ball; instead, watch the officials. Learn from their mistakes and successes.

Practice, of course, will help hone your instincts. Umpire a few games on the bases and soon you will unthinkingly get inside on base hits to the outfield, even if that move didn't come naturally for you on day one.

RULES KNOWLEDGE

The Old Days: In 1911 in Mobile, a batter named Johnny Bates hit a towering pop fly near second base. To the amazement of all, the ball lodged in the fuselage of a passing plane. The umpire ruled it a home-run, saying, "The last time I saw the ball, it was traveling out of the park in fair territory."

No doubt that play was not covered in the 1911 rulebook. So how to decide? At least one old-time umpire claimed he never read the rulebook. "The secret," he said, "was to figure out who screwed up, then make sure your ruling don't reward 'em."

That logic will get an umpire through most tough rule interpretations—but not all. And understanding that principle is no substitute for reading—studying!—the rulebook. You may sail through several games with no serious test of your rules knowledge. Then wham—batter's interference. You know someone on the offense should be called out, but is it the batter or the stealing runner?

Because some baseball and softball rules change every year, you need to stay *au courant* and read the book before the start of each season. And if you work both baseball and softball, you need to study each applicable rule book. For example, softball, high school baseball, and college baseball all have different catcher-interference rules.

Rule 9.01 of the professional rule book (and rule 10.1 of the softball book) gives umpires the authority to rule on any point not specifically covered in the rulebook. And there are plenty of points not specifically covered. Like this play I had while umpiring in spring training with the California Angels:

Batter Kenny Landreaux swung and missed for strike three. The ball entered the catcher's glove then popped back out, whereupon Landreaux's bat contacted it on the backswing, dribbling it down the first-base line. Because the catcher had not caught the strike three (and nobody was on first), Landreaux ran to first.

What's the correct call? Interference? Incidental contact?

Since Landreaux had not intentionally interfered, common sense suggested no interference. On the other hand, the catcher had been hindered in his attempt to catch the ball (it hadn't yet hit the ground), and interference does not have to be intentional. The point is, it's a close call and one you won't find spelled out in the rulebook. The umpire who faces such a call must interpret the applicable interference rule, weigh both sides, and reach a decision . . . now.

The award of bases after a ball goes out of play is well-covered in the rulebooks, yet it remains an area of confusion for umpires. In a game in the late thirties, with Whitey Witt on first base, the batter hit a line drive to the shortstop, who threw the ball into the stands trying to double up Whitey at first. Umpire Bill Gutherie motioned Witt to second.

Whitey protested, "No, I get two bases—I should go to third."

Gutherie shook his head. "I'm giving you two bases. One dis way (pointing toward first) and one dat way (pointing toward second)."

Today, all throws into dead territory result in two-base awards to the runners. The only issue is whether the award is made from the base the runner(s) attained at time of release or time of pitch. Consult your local rulebook for the game in your area.

JUDGMENT

Instructors can't teach judgment. We labor in hope that as our student-umpires grow more comfortable with their appearance and equipment, as they gain confidence with positioning, timing, et al, good judgment will eventually prevail.

That's usually true, but not always. As with all qualities discussed here, individual differences abound. Some people simply have bad judgment.

But not many.

Quiz

Try the following true/false test. Unless otherwise specified, questions apply to the two-umpire system at all levels of baseball and softball. The answers are on page 57.

1. If the third out of an inning is the result of a force play, no runs score on the play.

2. The base umpire makes all fair/foul calls.

3. The base umpire may wear white socks if he suffers from athlete's foot.

4. When finger-flashing signs to the base umpire, the plate umpire should give the count up and the number of outs down.

5. With a runner on 1st base and a base hit to the outfield, the plate umpire should move up the line toward 3rd and make any call there on the lead runner.

6. Bill Klem made his fame as the first president of the American League.

7. In most cases, the plate umpire should be in fair territory while making the call on a slide play at home.

8. The closer the play, the louder the umpire's voice.

9. When the batter interferes with the catcher's throw to 2nd, the umpire should call the stealing runner out.

10. During batter's interference, there is no penalty if the catcher throws out the stealing runner.

11. If the home team asks an umpire to sing the National Anthem, she should decline the offer.

12. When calling a game on account of bad weather, the umpire's main concern should be the safety of the participants.

13. Umpires should never change their calls.

14. On double plays, the base umpire is responsible for the calls at both 2nd and 1st.

15. Long ago, umpires ruled from the sidelines.

16. If they have good common sense, umpires don't need to read the rule book.

17. A runner is out for going (more than 3 feet) out of the baseline only if she does so to avoid a tag.

18. Because umpires don't want to call attention to themselves, flair is discouraged.

19. The plate umpire, even if he wears a mask, should wear a hat.

20. On plays at 1st, the umpire should use his ears as well as his eyes.

21. With nobody on base, the base umpire should set up 10-15 feet behind the first baseman, just in fair territory.

22. With nobody on base and a grounder to shortstop, the base umpire should make the call at 1st from foul territory.

23. The plate umpire should give the position of the pitch, as in "Ball one . . . outside."

24. If an argument, in the umpire's judgment, is personal or prolonged, he should eject the arguer.

25. A left-handed umpire may raise her left arm to signal strike.

26. Most rookie umpires find that their timing is too quick.

27. On the field, an umpire should never anticipate.

28. While moving into position to make a call, the umpire should always keep both eyes on the ball.

29. As the pitch is entering the catcher's glove, the plate umpire's head should be steady.

30. A good umpire will sometimes let a beefing ballplayer have the last word.

31. On force plays, the umpire should make the call as close to the play as possible without interfering.

32. The infield-fly sign (right hand across left chest) should be given to your partner with a runner on 1st and one out.

33. When calling a foul ball, the umpire should raise both arms upright and cry "foul."

34. When calling a fair ball, the umpire should point toward the infield and say nothing.

35. The umpire has the right to rule on any point not specifically covered in the rule book.

36. In most cases, the base umpire is responsible for the batter-runner all the way to 3rd base.

37. With nobody on base and a ground ball to the infield, the plate umpire should be moving toward 3rd.

38. When the ball is hit to the outfield, the base umpire should get inside the diamond.

39. There should be good eye contact between the plate and base umpires.

40. To steady the head, the plate umpire should go down on one knee when calling plays at the plate.

41. The umpire should insist that the players call him "Mr. Umpire."

42. The umpire with well-developed baseball instincts will empty his mind an instant before the pitch or play occurs.

43. Ideally, the umpire's voice and arm action for the strike call should be synchronized.

44. With a runner on 1st and one out, a fly ball is hit to right field for the second out. The throw to 1st to double off the runner sails into the stands. The proper award is the base the runner was going to (1st) plus the next base (2nd).

45. It is proper for the umpire to wear her hat backwards when she is wearing a mask.

46. The plate umpire should remove the mask (if wearing one) when the ball is hit.

47. If the umpire signals out but yells safe, the runner should be called safe.

48. When moving into position, the umpire should keep moving as he makes the call to get as close to the play as possible.

49. The umpire will have fewer arguments if he calls the close pitches strikes.

50. In place of a hat, the umpire may wear a headband.

Baseball and Fastpitch Softball

51. The umpire should call "ball" loudly right in the catcher's ear.

52. With runners on 1st and 2nd, a ground ball is hit to the shortstop, who throws to 3rd for the force. The call at 3rd belongs to the plate umpire.

53. When using the inside chest protector, the plate umpire should set up inside and one head above the catcher.

54. With runners on 1st and 2nd and a double steal, the base umpire is responsible for the call on both runners.

55. In baseball and fastpitch softball, positioning for the base umpire is the same.

Slowpitch Softball

56. If the batter moves up or back in the batter's box, the strike zone doesn't change for that particular batter.

57. The strike zone for a 5-foot batter and a 6-foot batter is the same as long as the arc and depth of the pitch are the same.

58. It is not necessary for the plate umpire to work the "slot."

59. Illegal pitches (under 6 feet and over 12 feet) should be called as soon as the umpire deems them illegal.

60. As a pitch is thrown, the base umpire should be in one of only two positions.

Answers

1. True
2. False. (If the base umpire is on the first-base line, he should call fair/foul on any ball hit past the first-base bag. Otherwise, the plate umpire makes fair/foul calls.)
3. False. (He can wear white socks beneath his dark socks.)
4. True
5. True. (Stay in foul territory; move into fair territory only if you actually make the call at 3rd.)
6. False
7. False
8. True
9. False. (Batter is out.)
10. True. (Ignore the interference.)
11. True
12. True
13. False. (When in doubt about a rule interpretation—as opposed to a judgment call—talk it over with your partner. If wrong, change the call to avoid a possible protest.)
14. True
15. True

16. False
17. True
18. False
19. True. (It's part of the uniform.)
20. True. (As a judge, you should gather all the evidence.)
21. False. (Stand just in foul territory.)
22. False. (From fair territory.)
23. False
24. True
25. False
26. True
27. False. (Anticipating ball/strike or out/safe is bad; anticipating how a play is developing is essential for good positioning.)
28. False. (Watch the ball, glance at the runner.)
29. True
30. True
31. False
32. False
33. True
34. True
35. True
36. True
37. False (Up the line toward 1st.)

38. True (Doing the pivot.)
39. True
40. False
41. False
42. True
43. True
44. False. (It's a two-base award—runner gets 3rd.)
45. False
46. True
47. False
48. False
49. True (But you must draw a fine line and be consistent.)
50. False
51. True
52. False
53. True
54. True
55. False (The baseball umpire works inside; the softball umpire outside.)
56. True. (The strike zone is an imaginary space over home plate, regardless of where the batter stands.)
57. False
58. True
59. True
60. True

Knotty Problems in Baseball History

8/22/1886: In the 11th inning of a game between the Cincinnati Reds and the Louisville Colonels, outfielder Abner Powell went back on a deep fly ball and was attacked by a dog. The mongrel latched onto Powell's leg like it was a soup bone. By the time Powell freed himself, the batter had circled the bases with the winning run.

(Do the modern rules mention canine interference?)

5/6/1892: Umpire Jack Sheridan stopped play between the scoreless Cincinnati and Boston teams in the 14th inning because the sun was at such an angle that it simultaneously blinded both the batter and pitcher. It was possibly the only time in baseball history that a game was called on account of sun.

(What criteria should umpires use in calling a game?)

8/7/06: The New York Giants forfeited a game to Chicago when manager John McGraw locked umpire James Johnston out of the ballpark. McGraw, who believed he "wasn't getting a fair shake" from Johnston, sent out one of his own players to umpire. The move was disallowed by the league president.

(Can an umpire eject a manager from outside the stadium?)

9/23/08: New York Giant player Fred Merkle became infamous for this play, known as "Merkle's Boner." Merkle was on first base when Al Bridwell hit what appeared to be the game-winning single against the Cubs. As the winning run scored, Merkle ran halfway to second, then turned and headed for the clubhouse. With thousands of fans milling about on the field, Cubs' second baseman Johnny Evers called for the ball and tagged second. Umpire Hank O'Day ruled Merkle out and disallowed the run. The Giants filed a protest, and the entire game was replayed two weeks later with the Cubs winning the game and the pennant.

(Why, according to the rulebook, did Merkle have to tag second?)

7/17/14: While legging out a triple, New York Giants outfielder Red Murray was struck by lightning, which dropped him between second and third. While lying there stunned, he was tagged out.

(Should an umpire ever call time to protect an injured player? Is time ever automatically out?)

6/8/20: Reds' centerfielder Edd Roush was ejected for taking a nap in the outfield. While his manager was arguing a call with umpire Bill Klem, Roush stretched out on the grass and fell asleep.

(Should he have been ejected for delay of game?)

7/26/35: New York's Jesse Hill hit into an unusual double play. His vicious line drive ricocheted off the head of Washington pitcher Ed Linke and flew back to catcher Jack Redmond, who caught it and threw to second to double off the runner who had failed to tag up.

(When could the runner legally tag up and leave?)

8/13/35: During a game in Cincinnati, the crowd became so unruly that a melee seemed likely. Umpire Beans Reardon tried to calm them with a personal speech that backfired. League president Ford Frick fined and reprimanded the umpires, and in so doing set the policy that exists today: The home team polices their stands and the umpires stay out of it.

(Why is it best that the umpires stay out of it?)

6/3/56: Nellie Fox of the Chicago White Sox was hit by two different pitches on the same at-bat. The first time that Fox was nailed by Oriole pitcher Johnny Schmitz, the plate umpire ruled he had made no attempt to get out of the way and thus did not get first base.

(What must a batter do to be awarded first base?)

6/7/57: A Brooklyn version of London's famed "pea soup" settled on Ebbets Field, forcing the umpires to call the game on account of fog.

(When is a lot of fog too much fog?)

6/23/63: Jimmy Piersall celebrated his one hundredth Major League home-run by circling the bases "back-first."

(Should the run count? What if he had run the bases in reverse order?)

7/29/65: In a Yankees-Twins game, the umpires took away an RBI single from Yankee catcher Thurman Munson when they found pine tar more than 18 inches up his bat handle.

(What's the rule on pine tar now?)

6/4/74: The umpires were forced to forfeit a game in Cleveland on 10-cent beer night. In the ninth inning with the score tied, unruly fans came onto the field and disrupted the game.

(At what point should umpires forfeit a game?)

5/27/81: Mets' third baseman Lenny Randle got down on his hands and knees to blow a slow roller foul.

(Foul ball? Interference?)

5/4/84: Oakland slugger Dave Kingman hit a towering pop fly that got stuck in the roof of the Metrodome.

(Ground-rule double? Home-run? Out? Know the ground rules before the game starts.)

4/16/2006: In a game between the Orioles and Angels, Miguel Tejada was on first with no outs. Javie Lopez hit a long fly ball to center. The centerfielder leaped at the fence but came up empty. He hit the wall so hard, he fell to the ground, the wind knocked out of him. In the meantime, Tejada, thinking the ball has been caught, headed back to first and passed Lopez, who correctly assumed it was a home-run.

(Who's out? Who scores?)

A Short History of Professional Umpiring

From the creation of base ball (originally two words) in the 1840s through the Civil War, the umpire was the personification of an amateur sport played by gentlemen. According to the 1845 rules of the Knickerbocker Club of New York, credited with creating modern baseball, the president of the club "shall appoint an Umpire, who shall keep the game in a book provided for that purpose, and note all violations of the Bylaws and Rules."

At first, three officials were used—one umpire chosen by each team and a neutral "referee" to decide the often partisan split decisions—but that didn't last long. In 1858 the National Association of Base Ball Players authorized a single umpire, sometimes a spectator or even a player, chosen by the home team with the consent of the opponent.

There was no dress code, but early umpires were distinguished-looking gentlemen—resplendent in top hat, Prince Albert coat, and cane—who stood, kneeled, or sat on a stool in foul territory along the first-base line. Early arbiters received no pay for their services, only the honor of being chosen "the sole judge of fair and unfair play."

Post-Civil War

As baseball gained popularity after the Civil War, both the game and the umpires gradually became more professional. In 1871, the newly formed National Association of Professional Base Ball Players continued to use unpaid volunteers. The home team was allowed to choose the umpire from a list of five names submitted by the visiting club. The umpire gained some autonomy when appeals were limited to rule interpretations, not judgment calls.

In 1878, the recently organized National League of Professional Base Ball Clubs instructed home teams to pay umpires $5 per game, and in 1879 National League president William A. Hulbert appointed baseball's first umpire staff—twenty men from which teams could chose one. Still, a cloud of suspicion hung over umpires. In 1882, Richard Higham was banished from the league for tipping off gamblers how to bet on games he officiated, the only professional umpire ever judged guilty of dishonesty on the field.

That same year a new professional league, the American Association, became the first to create an umpiring staff that was hired, paid ($140 per month), and assigned by the league itself. American Association umpires were required to wear blue flannel coats and caps on the field. The following year, the National League adopted its own permanent paid and uniformed staff.

Despite greater status, big league umpires in the nineteenth century led a stressful, and sometimes dangerous life. The game was changing rapidly—rules, equipment, playing techniques—making the umpire's job ever more difficult. And the physical and verbal abuse from fans, player, and coaches made it intolerable for some umpires. The men in blue were routinely spiked, kicked, cursed, and spat upon by players, while fans hurled insults and debris at them. Mobbings and physical assaults were common, as were police escorts for umpires.

Stereotyping the umpire-as-villain gained the support of club owners and league officials, who soon realized that umpire-baiting put people in the seats. To this end, they refused to support the umpires' decisions, paid their player's fines, turned a blind eye to rowdiness, and even joined sportswriters in scapegoating officials. Any umpire who retaliated—say, by hurling a bottle back into the stands or by punching a reporter—was fired.

The Twentieth Century

The 1903 agreement between the National League and the new American League brought Major League baseball into the modern era—and brought umpires greater stature and stability. Ban Johnson, president of the American League, gained a reputation for supporting his officials, which did much to boost their morale. He backed up his words by suspending players for flagrant misconduct. The National League soon followed Johnson's lead, and Major League umpires began to enjoy "unprecedented authority, dignity, and security."

Johnson also pushed for a second umpire on the field. Predictably, club owners resisted the added expense. Nevertheless, the use of two arbiters soon became standard—an umpire-in-chief to call balls and strikes and a field umpire to make calls on the bases. Again, the National League went along, and by 1912 both leagues had ten-man staffs—two umpires per game and two replacements in reserve.

Ban Johnson's men in blue developed a reputation for ability and character. To name just three: Senior umpire, Jack Sheridan, popularized working from a crouch position behind the plate; Billy Evans, in 1906, became the youngest Major League umpire in history; Tommy Connolly, English-born, umpired the American League's first game in 1901, and thirty years later became the first umpire-in-chief. Firm but patient, he seldom resorted to ejection, once going ten years without tossing anyone.

The National League had its own stars. Chief among them, Bill Klem, generally regarded as the greatest umpire in history. Intimidating and autocratic, Klem became infamous during arguments by towing a mark in the dirt and issuing a warning: "Don't cross the line!" He also pioneered the inside chest protector, the over-the-shoulder position for calling balls and strikes, and the raised right arm for strikes.

The Twenties & Thirties

Between World Wars I and II, when baseball dominated the nation's consciousness as the National Pastime, umpiring became a career for some men. Expanded schedules meant seven solid months of employment. Staffs became more stable, and an umpire who excelled the first two or three years could expect a long career. Umpires continued to endure arguments with players, insults from fans, and occasional flying objects, but the most vicious rowdiness declined. Stiff fines and suspensions were imposed for fighting and bottle tossing. In addition, abuse abated considerably after the infamous Black Sox Scandal, with the press elevating the umpire to a symbol of the game's integrity.

Although umpiring had become a more respectable vocation, no just system existed to determine who was hired and promoted. Becoming a professional umpire was mostly a matter of personal contacts, and advancement was more a matter of politics and personalities than merit. Still, the few who persevered and proved their worth enjoyed esteemed careers, if not high salaries.

Eventually, both major leagues established a pension plan for retired umpires who had served more than fifteen years. For their dedicated service, they received $100 per year with maximum lifetime benefits of $2,400.

The two-umpire system remained the standard during the 1920s, but more and more a third umpire was assigned to critical games. By 1933, three umpires were routinely assigned to work the regular season, and in 1952, the big leagues added a fourth umpire.

In the beginning, plate umpires in both leagues used inflated chest protectors. That forced them to call balls and strikes by crouching directly behind the catcher and looking over his head. While the American League continued to use the "balloon" protector, National League umpires followed Bill Klem's lead and adopted the more compact inside chest protector, which allowed them to work "the slot," just over the catcher's shoulder nearest the batter. Due to those positioning differences, American League umpires developed a reputation for calling more high strikes, and National Leaguers for calling more low strikes.

Umpire Schools

The first umpire training schools were established in the 1930s. By the mid-1950s training-school graduates were common in the Major Leagues, and by the 1960s it was nearly impossible to umpire in pro ball without attending a training school.

The schools elevated umpiring to a new level. Graduates were better versed in the rules and more skilled in techniques than earlier self-taught umpires. Formal training also created a uniformity of style and personality, as students were instructed "by the book."

Radical Changes

In 1966, twenty years after Jackie Robinson broke the color line, baseball finally promoted a black umpire, Emmett Ashford, to the American League. In 1973 Art Williams integrated the National League. American League umpires Armando Rodriguez (1974) and Rich Garcia (1975) were the first Hispanic umpires in the majors.

Early efforts by umpires to unionize were ineffective and risky. In 1945, Ernie Stewart of the American League was fired for alleged unionizing activity. Finally, in 1963, led by Augie Donatelli, umpires organized the National League Umpires Association. After their success in obtaining raises, American League umpires, too, joined the union.

In 1968, umpires Bill Valentine and Al Salerno were dismissed, allegedly for incompetence but more likely for unionizing activities. In response, umpires in both leagues organized into the Major League Umpires Association.

After a one-day strike of the first game of the playoffs, in 1970, the first ever by Major League umpires, the league presidents recognized the Association and negotiated a labor contract that set a minimum salary of $11,000 and an average salary of $21,000.

Two more umpire strikes followed in the 1970s, leading to major concessions for the union, including a salary range of $22,000 to $55,000, based on years of service; annual no-cut contracts; and two weeks' midseason vacation. The strikes created ill will between the union umpires and the four "scab" umpires retained on each league's staff.

Television

The umpire's union owes much of its success to the power of television, which generated unprecedented revenues. Once televised games became popular in the early 1950s, a few umpires played to the camera, most notably Emmett Ashford and Ron Luciano. Luciano, famous for "shooting" runners out on the bases, even leveraged his notoriety into a career as a broadcaster and writer.

The personal lives of umpires also received more scrutiny. In 1988 Commissioner Giamatti, at the behest of club owners, released ten-year National League umpire Dave Pallone out of fear that his homosexuality might tarnish baseball's image. National League president Bill White forced umpire Bob Engel to retire after his conviction for shoplifting baseball cards. And in 1991, two unidentified umpires received a year's probation for alleged contacts with bookmakers, even though no evidence suggested they'd ever bet on baseball games.

In 1971, American League umpires adopted gray slacks and maroon blazers, an attempt to project a sportier image. To that end, umpires in both leagues soon began wearing numerals on their sleeves and baseball caps with letters designating league affiliation. Today, umpires usually wear short-sleeved shirts without jackets during hot weather and satin warm-up jackets on cool nights.

Eyeglasses were discouraged until 1991 when Al Clark (AL) and Frank Pulli (NL) wore them on the field. In 1988 obese umpires were put on weight-reduction programs during the off season, and those who failed to lose weight risked suspension. My instructor at umpire school, National League umpire John McSherry, was both obese and highly respected for his skills. He died on the field in 1995.

Conclusion

In 1999, the Major League Umpires Association, led by Richie Phillips, urged its members to resign, a power play aimed at forcing Major League Baseball to the bargaining table. When it backfired, twenty-two umpires had lost their careers. They tried to rescind their resignation, but Baseball wouldn't take them back.

After much heartache, bitterness, and legal wrangling, at least half of the twenty-two umps were rehired, and others eventually received severance pay.

Despite such setbacks, and some high-publicity blown calls, professional umpires have continued to gain respectability—and raises. As of this writing, Major League umpire salaries range from about $84,000 to $300,000 per year.

In a hundred-plus years of baseball, the umpire has morphed from gentleman arbiter to untrained "necessary evil" to skilled professional who epitomizes the integrity of the game itself.

You Make the Call

Ten Tough Calls for Umpires at Any Level

1. Runner on first base is stealing. As the batter swings at the pitch, his bat contacts the catcher's mitt.

2. With a runner on second, batter hits a hard groundball to shortstop. The runner, moving toward third, has to slow to avoid being hit by the batted ball. The ball, in fact, just misses the runner, and the shortstop kicks it for an error.

3. Runner on first and a groundball to the second baseman. The throw to first goes into the dugout.

4. Batter hits a foul fly ball near the visitor's bench. First baseman moves over, makes the catch in live territory, then her momentum carries her across the chalk line separating live and dead territory.

5. With the bases empty, batter hits a ground ball to short. When the throw takes the first baseman off the bag, she attempts to sweep-tag the batter-runner. Who makes the call in the two-umpire system?

6. Runners on second and third, and a fly ball to center. Both runners tag and move up one base. The defense appeals that both runners left too early.

7. Runner on first, who is stealing, gets caught in a rundown. While in the baseline, the runner turns and contacts a fielder who does not have the ball.

8. Runner on first, fly ball to deep left field. Runner, thinking the ball will be caught, retreats to first to tag. As the ball hits off the fielder's glove, the batter-runner rounds first, passing the tagging runner.

9. No runners on and a sinking liner to centerfield. The outfielder charges and either makes the catch or short-hops it—it's tough to tell.

10. Bases loaded, no outs, and a pop fly to the shortstop.

Answers

1. Ask yourself, “Who screwed up?” Answer: the defense. Since the offense may benefit more from the play than the penalty, let the play go. Do not call time immediately. If the batter and all runners advance at least one base, ignore the interference. If not, call time and enforce the penalty: the batter gets first base. But do any runners advance? Consult your rulebook, as this part of the rule varies by sport and level.

2. No interference. The runner must avoid being hit by a batted ball, lest he be called out for interference. That may require slowing down or speeding up, which is sometimes enough to distract a fielder. Unless the runner did something intentional or out of the ordinary to interfere with the fielder, let the play go.

3. As soon as the ball enters dead territory, the plate umpire should raise both arms and yell, “Dead ball.” Any partners should mimic the call, stopping any hell-bent runners. Repeat as necessary. Then, immediately and with great command, make your awards, pointing the runners to their allotted bases. And know those awards cold.

Throws that go out of play (except from a pitcher on the rubber) are always two-base awards. It's simply a matter of whether the award is made from the base attained at the time of the a) pitch or b) release. Consult the rulebook for the particular sport.

4. As soon as the fielder carries the caught ball into dead territory, the plate umpire should raise both arms and cry, "Dead ball!" Then immediately and forcefully award any runners one base beyond the base they had at the time of the pitch.

5. With no runners on, the plate umpire should move up the first-base line, halfway if possible. The base umpire makes the initial call at first, but if you don't see it well and if one team erupts, consider going to your partner for help. If you do that, it's best to go immediately and forcefully: "Did he get him?!" And the plate ump's reply should be in an equally stentorian tone—"Yes, he did!"— synchronized with a dynamic out call. Put all those pieces together—hustling plate umpire, dynamic communication, and, if necessary, quick reversal—and the umpire crew comes out of a tough situation looking very good indeed.

6. First, the defense can indeed appeal both bases. With few exceptions, the base umpire is responsible for watching the touches and tags at first and second base; the plate umpire has third and home. If a runner leaves too soon or misses a bag, the umpires say nothing unless the defense properly appeals. Except in slowpitch softball, the pitcher must put the ball in play. Once that is accomplished without a balk or illegal pitch, the appropriate umpire makes the call. You should have been in position to see it, but if you weren't, call the runners safe. Never guess "out."

7. Obstruction. Ask: Who screwed up? Answer: the defense. Since the offense may benefit more from the play than the penalty, delay calling time. But most often, the play grinds to a halt, and everyone turns to the umpire for clarity. Call time, yell, "Obstruction!" and make awards. Consult your rulebook, as some levels of play always advance the runner while others award the base to which the runner was heading—in this case, first base.

8. Who screwed up? Answer: the offense. Normally, if the offense errs, you kill the play immediately, under the assumption that the offense may not benefit from the play. This play is an exception.

Immediately raise your right arm, point to the batter-runner, and call her out. But do not raise both arms and kill the play unless that is the third out of the inning. Otherwise, let the play go, as the tagging runner may still advance or be thrown out.

9. In the two-umpire system, with the bases empty, the plate umpire should hustle out into fair territory, generally toward the ball but at an angle to maximize his view. On a close catch/no-catch, make the call as quickly as possible, selling it with voice and flair. If one side erupts in anger, consider taking your partner aside for a conference. If your partner saw it no better than you did, stick with the original call.

10. The infield-fly rule is in effect. The batter is out, but time is in. Delay the "out" call a moment if you have any doubt whether the ball can be caught "with ordinary effort." (Note: ordinary effort varies greatly according to skill level) Once the plate umpire decides "yes" (and the defense dropping it does not necessarily make that a bad decision), he should raise his right arm, making the out call, while shouting, "Batter is out!" two or more times.

The base umpire should mimic the out call. If the pop fly is then dropped, both umpires should repeat the out call loudly. Remember, time is not out. The runners can advance at their own risk, although they must tag up if the ball is caught.

Some Umpire Records

- Most seasons as a Major League umpire: Bill Klem, 37

- Most World Series: Bill Klem, 18

- Most World Series games: Bill Klem, 108

- Most All-Star games: Al Barlick and Bill Summers, 7

- Most consecutive games umpired: George Hildebrand, 3,510

- First black professional umpire: Emmett Ashford, 1951

- First black Major League umpire, Ashford, 1966

- First Hispanic Major League umpire: Armando Rodriguez, 1974

- First female professional umpire: Bernice Gera, 1972 (one game in the Class A New York-Penn League)

- First trained female professional umpire: Pam Postema (thirteen years in the minors)

- Youngest Major League umpire: Billy Evans, 22

- Oldest Major League umpire: Bill Klem, 68.

Umpires Enshrined in the Baseball Hall of Fame

- Tommy Connolly (1901-1931)
- Bill Klem (1905-1941)
- Billy Evans (1906-1927)
- Bill McGowan (1925-54)
- Al Barlick (1940-1971)
- Jocko Conlan (1941-1964)
- Cal Hubbard (1946-1951)
- Nestor Chylak (1954-1978)
- Doug Harvey (1962-1992)

Quotes by and About Umpires

"It's not easy to be an umpire and a Negro too. Maybe Sammy Davis would have a more difficult problem. He's a Negro too, but he only has one eye." –American League umpire Emmett Ashford

"Umpires are most vigorous when defending their miscalls." –Jim Brosnan

"They expect an umpire to be perfect on Opening Day and to improve as the season goes on." –American League umpire Nestor Chylak

"The best thing about umpiring is seeing the best in baseball every day. The cardinal rule of umpiring is to follow the ball wherever it goes. Well, if you watch the ball, you can't help seeing somebody make a great catch . . . That's what makes umpiring so much fun." –National League umpire Shag Crawford

“You argue with the umpire because there is nothing else you can do about it.” –Leo Durocher

“As a whole, the managers today are different in temperament. Most have very good communication skills and are more understanding of the umpire's job. That doesn't mean they are better managers. It just means that I perceive today's managers a bit differently.” –Major League umpire Jim Evans

“Professional managers, coaches, and players have a right to question an umpire's decision if they do it in a professional manner. When they become personal, profane, or violent, they have crossed the line and must be dealt with accordingly.” –Jim Evans

“Most plays that are missed by the umpire are caused by the umpire not reading those cues early enough and making the proper adjustments.” –Jim Evans

“Take pride in your work at all times. Remember, respect for an umpire is created off the field as well as on.” –Ford Frick

“One of the really wrong theories about officiating is that a good official is one you never notice. The umpire who made that statement was probably a real poor official who tried to get his paycheck and hide behind his partners and stay out of trouble all his life. Control of the ballgame is the difference between umpires that show up for the players and the managers.” –National League umpire Bruce Froemming

“It isn't enough for an umpire merely to know what he's doing. He has to look as though he know what he's doing too.” –National League umpire Larry Goetz

“Boys, I'm one of those umpires that misses 'em every once in a while so if it's close, you'd better hit it.” –Cal Hubbard

“Being an umpire wasn't such a tough job. You really have to understand only two things and that's maintaining discipline and knowing the rule book.” –Cal Hubbard

"When I first went into the American League, Johnny Rice told me that the toughest call an umpire has to make is not the half-swing. The toughest call is throwing a guy out of the game after you blew the hell out of the play." –American League umpire Bill Kinnamon

"Umpire's heaven is a place where he works third base every game. Home is where the heartache is." –American League umpire Ron Luciano

"Any umpire who claims he never missed a call is . . . well, an umpire." –Ron Luciano

"Umpires are human, too—as we are finding out." –Steve Lyons

"Why is it they boo me when I call a foul ball correctly and they applaud the starting pitcher when he gets taken out of the ballgame?" –American League umpire Jerry Neudecker

"Fans and players boo and abuse umpires, but there isn't one umpire in the history of baseball who has ever been proved guilty of being dishonest. I've very proud to have been an umpire." –American League umpire George Pipgras

"Wanting to be an umpire is tantamount to wanting to be President of the United States. I can admire their fierce sense of responsibility, whether they are right or wrong, but sometimes it comes down to being a thankless job; however, the job must be done." –Art Rust in *Recollections of a Baseball Junkie* (1985)

"I didn't mean to hit the umpire with the dirt, but I did mean to hit that bastard in the stands." –Babe Ruth

"The umpire must be quick witted. He may not, like the wise old owl of the bench, look over his gold-rimmed eye-glasses, inform the assembled multitude that he will 'take the matter under advisement,' and then adjourn the court for a week or two to satisfy himself how he ought to decide. No, indeed. He must be johnny-on-the-spot with a decision hot off the griddle and he must stick to it, right or wrong—or be lost." –A.G. Spalding in *America's National Game* (1911)

"The worst thing about umpiring (in professional baseball) is the loneliness. It's a killer. Every city is a strange city. You don't have a home. Ballplayers are home fifty percent of the them, umpires are not." –American League umpire Ernie Stewart

"The thing that surprised me most in baseball is the amount of integrity that most umpires have. It actually took me a while to believe what a good game they'd give you the next night after a blow-up." –Earl Weaver

"If they did get a machine to replace us, you know what would happen to it? Why, the players would bust it to pieces every time it ruled against them. They'd clobber it with a bat." –National League umpire Harry Wendelstadt

"Why are the umpires, the only two people on the field who aren't going to get grass stains on their knees, the only ones allowed to wear dark trousers?" –Katharine Whitehorn

Bill Klem Quotes

Bill Klem, who many claim was the greatest umpire ever, may also have been the most quotable arbiter. Here is a sampling of his remarks.

“An angry player can't argue with the back of an umpire who is walking away.”

“Baseball is more than a game to me, it's a religion.”

“Fix your eye on the ball from the moment the pitcher holds it in his glove. Follow it as he throws to the plate and stay with it until the play is completed. Action takes place only where the ball goes.”

“Gentleman, he was out because I said he was out.” (Statement made after being shown a photo of a blown call.)

“It ain't nothin' till I call it.”

“That guy in a twenty-five cent bleacher seat is as much entitled to know a call as the guy in the boxes. He can see my arm signal even if he can't hear my voice.”

"The best umpired game is the game in which the fans cannot recall the umpires who worked it."

"The most cowardly thing in the world is blaming mistakes upon the umpires. Too many managers strut around on the field trying to manage the umpires instead of their teams."

"There are one-hundred fifty-four games in a season and you can find one-hundred fifty-four reasons why your team should have won every one of them."

"Your job is to umpire for the ball and not the player."

Suggested Reading

The Umpire Strikes Back
Ron Luciano

Humorous observations about the umpiring life.

The Fall of the Roman Umpire
Ron Luciano

More of the same.

The Best Seat in Baseball but You Have to Stand: The Game as the Umpires See it
Lee Gutkind

The author traveled with a National League umpire crew during the 1974 season.

The Men in Blue: Conversations with Umpires
Larry R. Gerlach

Major League umpires up close and personal.

As They See 'Em: A Fan's Travels in the Land of Umpires
Bruce Weber

A baseball devotee goes to an umpire school and then wherever umpire stories take him.

Strrr-ike!!: Emmett Ashford, Major League Umpire
Adrienne Cherie Ashford

The life story of the first black umpire in the Major Leagues, as told by his daughter.

Online Resources

http://mlb.mlb.com/mlb/official_info/umpires/roster.jsp

Everything you want to know about Major League umpires.

http://www.naso.org/BeOfficial/sportspages/baseball.html

This National Association of Sports Officials (NASO) site is the starting place for officials in most amateur sports, including baseball and softball.

http://web.minorleaguebaseball.com/milb/info/umpires.jsp?mc=_ump_history

Umpiring in the minor leagues revealed.

http://www.majorleagueumpires.com/umpire_schools.htm

All about the umpire schools for professional baseball.

http://www.collegiatebaseball.com/umpiring/umpirelinks.htm

Full of links to sites about umpires and umpiring.

http://www.sdabu.com/history_main.htm

An engaging history of umpiring.

DVDs

"You Be the Judge: An Introduction to Basic Umpiring Skills"
Steve Boga, producer/writer

Designed to accompany this book, "You Be the Judge" is still the best video training program available for baseball and softball officials at all levels. Ideal for umpires and for umpire trainers.

Photo Courtesy of UPI

CPSIA information can be obtained at www.ICGtesting.com
Printed in the USA
LVOW10s1356070415

433608LV00001B/134/P